T0648435

Galley Guide
for
Gourmets

Galley Guide for Gourmets

TEMPTING TOP-OF-THE-RANGE DISHES
FROM BOXES AND CANS

FERNE RAVESON
With illustrations by the author

DODD, MEAD & COMPANY · NEW YORK

This volume is a completely revised and
expanded edition of the book originally
published under the title *Galley Gourmet*

TO MY SKIPPER

Contents

ON BOARD RECIPES

MEATS

FOWL

FISH

SIDE DISHES

BREADS

DESSERTS

A Note to First Mates

Galley Guide for Gourmets is the offspring of *Galley Gourmet,* my first book, written a few years ago for all first mates, on land and on sea. It was put together then to fill the need for easy gourmet techniques to be used in the confines of the average yacht galley or any other place where cooking facilities and/or fresh food ingredients were limited. The recipes, let me say immodestly, have been well received.

And now, *Galley Guide for Gourmets* has been written with the same goal in mind—to help you prepare gourmet meals in short-order time from boxes and cans and without the benefit of an oven or other modern kitchen conveniences. In the *Guide,* I have repeated earlier recipes, several of which have been revised, and have added many new ones. They have all been galley tested, are easy to prepare, tempt-

ing and tasty. More important, they are guaranteed not to turn your main cabin into a Turkish steam bath!

Galley Guide for Gourmets is a compilation of my best on-board recipes and unusual but simple dishes to make ahead of time and take on board. This "Make and Take" section, which proved so popular in the first book, has been greatly expanded and includes a variety of dishes especially good for entertaining at home as well as at sea.

So get away from the usual shipboard fare and be a gourmet, not a slave, in your galley. You'll love the results, love the extra free time on deck, and love the admiration of the skipper and crew, who will love you even more!

Good luck and happy sailing.

On Improving Your Meals

Serve wine with your dinners as often as possible. It's easy to stow and lends elegance to the plainest meal. Also, wine is probably the most important ingredient you can add to canned meats so they won't taste as though they came out of a can.

Keep a good supply of fresh and minced dried onions aboard. Fresh onions keep well without refrigeration. Try both fresh and dry in some dishes.

Carry beef and chicken bouillon cubes or powder—especially handy for recipes calling for ½ cup of broth.

Cut or tear green salad ingredients at home. Carry to boat and refrigerate in tightly covered plastic containers or plastic bags, without dressing. Will keep for several days this way. Saves space, eliminates work on board, and cuts down on garbage.

For intriguing green salads, try adding one or more of the following: bacon bits, Mandarin oranges, pineapple chunks, marinated artichokes, garlic croutons, chopped chives, minced onions, pecans, or melon balls. Serve with tarragon vinegar and oil, with a dash of garlic salt and pepper.

Powdered milk these days is both convenient and more pleasing to a discerning milk drinker. Increase the proportions to almost half milk, half water for a more full-bodied texture and taste. Shake well and be sure to serve it cold.

Carry a variety of envelopes of gravy mixes to add to the natural juices of canned meats.

Serve whole cranberry sauce mixed with chutney as relish with pork, turkey, or chicken.

You will note the use of a cream substitute in several recipes in this book. Start your trip with it in frozen form and it will conveniently last for three weeks in the icebox after defrosting. Some brands taste more like cream than others; experiment until you find the one you like best.

Packaged frozen meats are wonderful to start a trip with and will keep for two or three days on ice. Frozen fish, however, should be used immediately upon thawing.

Carry a good selection of seasonings and herbs for "doctoring" canned foods. Your selection might include Worcestershire sauce, garlic powder, Jane's Krazy Mixed-Up Salt, curry powder, paprika, chopped chives, bacon bits, basil, nutmeg, cinnamon, ginger, oregano, chili powder, tarragon, and parsley flakes.

If there's room aboard, a pressure cooker is extremely helpful, especially when out on a long trip and fresh meats are available.

For extended trips, consider taking along your electric frying pan and toaster-oven to plug in at dockside when possible.

On Making Sandwiches

There are good sandwiches, bad sandwiches, and sandwiches that fall into neither category. Since this is one of the most convenient and acceptable ways to serve lunch on a boat, sandwiches deserve a section all their own.

For a change, and for especially attractive lunches, try serving open-faced Danish style sandwiches. (These also are a boon to weight watchers.) Use the square, thinly sliced, packaged pumpernickel usually found refrigerated in the dairy department of your supermarket. Spread this delicious bread with butter, and then—almost anything goes! Even ham-and-cheese looks and tastes better this way; but try other cold cuts, as well as leftover meats (roast beef, chicken, pork, turkey, veal, etc.), tuna fish, small shrimp, egg salad, liver paste with mushrooms, sardines, sliced eggs, pickled herring, ad infinitum! Add mustard and mayonnaise where appropriate and decorate imaginatively, using green pepper, pimiento, canned sliced tomatoes, pickles, olives, or perhaps a thin, twisted slice of cucumber or orange. Or try pickled beet slices on each side of the curled cucumber over a bed of egg salad; or use the leftover breakfast bacon on top of the liver paste and add a few sliced mushrooms for taste as well as looks.

Or, how about spreading thin pumpernickel slices with smoked-salmon-flavored whipped cream-cheese and topping with thin sliced tomatoes sprinkled with dried minced onions and bacon bits? Better still, butter thin pumpernickel and spread it with mayonnaise. Then, add canned kippers, sliced hard-boiled eggs (season with pepper and Jane's

17

Krazy Salt), and top all with thin slices of onion. And for easy but elegant hors d'oeuvres, try cutting the pumpernickel into small squares. Spread with a mixture of whipped cream-cheese and butter and add a dab of red or black caviar to each square (alternate with both for a colorful platter). The combinations are literally endless!

The ordinary lunch box sandwich need not be ordinary. Remember to moisten your sandwiches with butter, margarine, or mayonnaise—stale bread is taboo. When making fillings, add minced onions, chopped chives, or bacon bits to give zest to the usually bland egg or tuna fish salad. And try adding a tablespoon or two of chutney to tuna fish salad. It's deliciously different!

Don't forget to sprinkle seasoning on leftover meat; onion salt and pepper go a long way to make up for the tasty gravy that went with it the night before. Try varying the sandwich bread, using rye, pumpernickel, or whole wheat, as well as the many varieties of white to be found on today's market shelf. And it helps to serve some olives, pickles, or chunks of cheese on the side, along with corn or potato chips. But most of all, strive to serve *attractive* sandwiches, for food that looks good usually tastes better, too.

Highly Recommended

Wilson's canned meats—Pork, Beef, Turkey, Corned Beef, and Ham. Recipe on beef can for "Bordeaux Gravy" is excellent. Also, try "Gravy Supreme" recipe on pork can.

Hormel's "Famous Foods of the World"—Kottbullar, Beef Stroganoff, and Chicken Cacciatora. Serve over rice or noodles.

Betty Crocker Noodles Romanoff, Italiano, or Stroganoff. Also, Betty Crocker Rice Provence and Rice Milanese. (Use top-of-stove method.)

Rice-A-Roni, Beef and Chicken.

Uncle Ben's Quick Rice. Also, Uncle Ben's Long Grain and Wild Rice with Selected Herbs and Seasonings.

French's Chili-O-Mix. Follow directions on package. Good to "Make and Take," too.

French's Potato Pancake Mix. (Add 2 tablespoons dried minced onion.)

Milani's Newburg Sauce.

S. S. Pierce foods, especially Swedish Meatballs, Meatballs in Tomato Sauce (add oregano, garlic, and 3 tablespoons tomato paste), and Stuffed Cabbage. Most all of these are excellent right from the can, but a few extra spices make them even better.

Canned precooked bacon, frankfurters, sliced salad tomatoes, date and nut bread, brown bread, and jars of cheese, all of which do not require refrigeration.

Doxsee Clam Dip and Minced Clams.

"Make and Take"

*Unless otherwise noted,
all recipes in this book
serve 4.*

ANN'S BEEF SALAD

1 pound ground round steak
1 teaspoon each chili powder
  and Jane's Krazy Salt
1 small head lettuce
1 cucumber
1 pound cherry tomatoes
1 red onion, sliced
1 green pepper, cut coarsely

1 ripe avocado, sliced
½ pound package shredded
  cheddar cheese
2 tablespoons dried minced
  onions
1 jar Thousand Island salad
  dressing
Dorita Corn Chips, plain

Brown meat with chili powder and Jane's Salt. Pack in separate container. Shred lettuce and pack in another container with cucumber (peel, slice lengthwise, scoop out center, and slice), whole tomatoes, sliced onion, and green pepper. Just before serving, combine greens, and meat. Peel and slice avocado, add shredded cheddar, minced onions and toss with dressing. Crush about ¾ of the chips over salad and toss once again, lightly. A complete and delicious meal served with garlic bread. Serves 6.

23

BEEF BURGUNDY

3 pounds chuck, roast or steak
Herb marinade (recipe below)
2 tablespoons each salad oil
   and butter or margarine
1 cup chopped onions
2 garlic cloves, minced
1½ cups Burgundy wine

2 10½-ounce cans beef
   bouillon
1-pound can small whole
   onions
¾ pound mushrooms
2 tablespoons flour
3 tablespoons rice flour

Trim meat and cut into 1″ cubes. Pour marinade over meat in bowl, cover and let stand in refrigerator overnight (no longer than 24 hours); stir once or twice. Drain marinade, discard, and brown meat quickly in oil and margarine. Add onion and garlic, reduce heat, and cook until onion is soft. Add wine and bouillon, cover, and simmer for 1½ hours or until meat is tender. Drain canned onions, reserving liquid. Add onions and mushrooms to pan and cook 10 minutes longer. Gradually add flour and rice flour to ½ cup of the onion liquid and mix until smooth. Stir into pan and stir constantly until gravy thickens, but do not boil. Serve with salad and chunks of French bread for mopping up gravy. Serves 6 to 8.

HERB MARINADE

Thoroughly blend 2 tablespoons salad oil, 1 teaspoon salt, ½ teaspoon each pepper and thyme, and 1 crushed bay leaf. Add 2 cups Burgundy or other dry red wine and stir.

BEEF LA COMIDA

1½ pounds chuck or stew beef
3 tablespoons oil
¼ teaspoon each salt and
   pepper
¼ teaspoon garlic powder
¼ cup dried onions
1 cup water
½ cup chutney
2 teaspoons Worcestershire
   sauce

dash of tabasco
1 crushed bay leaf
1 bouillon cube
2 tablespoons extra dry aperatif
   (Pikina if possible)
¼ cup slivered almonds
¾ cup long-grained rice
1 teaspoon paprika

Brown chunks of meat in oil and season with paprika, salt, pepper, garlic, and onions. Mix ½ cup water with chutney, Worcestershire, tabasco, and bay leaf and add to skillet. Reduce heat and cook for one hour or until meat is tender. (Stir about every 10 minutes and watch that gravy doesn't boil away.) Add aperatif, ½ cup more water, bouillon cube, almonds, and rice. Stir well and cook on low heat 25 minutes longer and add boiled water if needed.

25

BEEF PILAU

2 pounds boneless chuck,
  cubed
2 tablespoons oil
3 teaspoons dried onion
1 teaspoon Jane's Krazy Salt
¼ teaspoon pepper

½ teaspoon garlic salt
1 can onion soup
½ cup dry red wine
boiled water as needed
1 cup Quick Rice

Brown meat in oil. Add seasonings, onion soup, and wine
and simmer 1 hour. When meat is tender, be sure there has
been enough boiled water added to make about 1½ cups
of gravy. Add rice and cook 5 minutes longer.

BRISKET WITH SAUERKRAUT
AND RAISINS

3- or 4-pound brisket
2 tablespoons oil
1 large onion, sliced
1 #2 can sauerkraut
1-pound can tomatoes
1 can tomato paste

2 garlic cloves, sliced
¼ cup sugar
1 tablespoon paprika
salt and pepper to taste
½ cup raisins

Trim meat and brown in oil. Add onion and brown lightly. Add rest of ingredients except raisins. Cover and cook over low heat for 2 hours or until meat is tender. Add raisins 15 minutes before roast is finished. Slicing meat at home is most helpful.

MEATBALLS IN
CRANBERRY-CHILI SAUCE

1½ pounds ground chuck
1 package dried onion soup
1 egg
½ box Uneeda Biscuits

1 head cabbage
1 can whole cranberry sauce
1 bottle chili sauce

Add onion soup, egg, and water-soaked Uneeda Biscuits to meat. Blend well and form into medium sized balls. Line bottom of large deep pan with chunks of cabbage, cover with meatballs and add cranberry and chili sauce. Cover and bake in 350° oven for 2 hours. Stir for smoother gravy. Serves 6 to 8.

SEAFARING STEAK 'N SAUCE

2–3 pounds flank steak
Sally Levy's marinade (recipe below)

Marinate steak or steaks in 1 cup of sauce in covered container and store in refrigerator overnight. Remove meat and broil, basting with sauce frequently. Cook, slice, and store in container with at least ½ cup sauce and serve hot or cold. An especially tasty "Make and Take."

NB: Any leftover sauce may be returned to its original container for reuse.

SALLY LEVY'S MARINADE

3 cans tomato sauce
  (8-ounce size)
¾ cup each:
  white vinegar
  tarragon vinegar
  dry white wine
6 tablespoons honey

6 tablespoons soy sauce
1 tablespoon salt
¾ teaspoon each:
  ground rosemary
  powdered ginger
  ground basil
6 garlic cloves

Mix all ingredients and simmer for ten minutes. Let cool and remove garlic cloves.

This recipe will keep for 2 months under refrigeration and is excellent as a barbecue sauce as well as a marinade.

BIG ISLAND STEW

2 pounds ground beef	1 can (32-ounce) tomatoes
1 green pepper, chopped	1 can string beans
2 onions, sliced	1 tablespoon steak sauce
¼ cup oil	basil
1 can red kidney beans	dried mustard
1 can whole corn	salt and pepper

Brown ground beef, green pepper, and onions in oil. Add all vegetables, steak sauce, a pinch of basil and dried mustard, and salt and pepper to taste. Cook 20 to 25 minutes.

LAMB A L'ANN

1½ pounds fresh string beans
2 pounds lamb, cubed
3 tablespoons oil
1 large onion, diced
2–3 garlic cloves

2 10-ounce cans Italian
  tomatoes
1 tablespoon sugar
½ teaspoon Jane's Krazy
  Mixed-Up Salt
Salt and pepper to taste

Clean string beans and snip off ends but leave whole. Brown lamb in oil. Add onion and minced garlic and cook until golden. Add beans, stir in tomatoes and seasonings and simmer for 1½ to 2 hours, stirring occasionally. Serve with rice.

LAMB IMPERIAL

2 pounds boneless lamb
  shoulder
3 tablespoons oil
2 tablespoons butter or
  margarine
2 onions, diced
1 cup uncooked long grain rice
1 teaspoon salt

½ teaspoon pepper
½ teaspoon nutmeg
½ cup white raisins
1 can chicken broth
3 tablespoons Realemon juice
boiling water
½ cup toasted almonds

Brown cubed lamb in oil and remove from pan. Lower heat, melt butter and add onions and rice. Stir and cook until rice is opaque. Mix in salt, pepper, nutmeg, raisins, broth and lemon juice, then replace meat in pan. Simmer 45 minutes or until meat is tender, adding boiling water as needed to keep rice moist. Garnish with almonds. Serves 6.

CHUTNIED LAMB

½ leg of lamb
2 garlic cloves
Jane's Krazy Mixed-Up Salt
salt and pepper
3 heaping tablespoons chutney

½ cup dry white wine
2 tablespoons Worcestershire
    sauce
slivered almonds

Make several deep slits in meat with paring knife. Slice garlic cloves and insert into the slits. Sprinkle roast with Jane's Salt, salt and pepper, and then spread chutney on top. Add wine and bake in 350° oven for 2 hours, basting every 15 minutes or so. When done, pour off gravy into saucepan. Mix flour with ½ cup of the gravy, return to saucepan, add Worcestershire, and stir over medium heat until thickened. Correct seasoning if needed. Slice meat ahead of time and carry to boat with gravy in separate container. Reheat and serve with almonds.

RIJSTTAFEL
(Curried Veal)

2–3 pounds cubed veal
3 tablespoons oil
1 stalk celery
1 large onion, sliced
2 cans Franco-American Beef
  Gravy

1 teaspoon salt
½ teaspoon pepper
1 tablespoon Worcestershire
  sauce
1 tablespoon curry powder

Brown veal in oil. Add enough water to just about cover meat, cover and simmer 1 hour. In separate pan, brown celery and sliced onion. Add to veal plus the 2 cans of gravy, salt, pepper, Worcestershire, and curry. Simmer for another hour. Serve over rice with 3 or 4 condiments. (Always chutney and raisins; chopped nuts, crumbled bacon, shredded coconut, chopped hard-cooked eggs, etc.) Serves 6 to 8.

CHICKEN CHARLOTTE

thighs and breasts for 4
salt and pepper
flour
2 tablespoons butter or
  margarine
2 tablespoons oil
2 onions, diced

1 green pepper, diced
½ teaspoon garlic powder
1½ teaspoon curry powder
½ teaspoon thyme
1 large can stewed tomatoes
½ cup raisins
¼ cup white wine

Coat chicken parts with flour, salt and pepper. Brown in butter and oil, remove from skillet and arrange in casserole dish. If necessary, add butter to skillet and lightly brown onions and green pepper. Add the garlic, curry, thyme, tomatoes, raisins, and wine and simmer 10 minutes. Pour over chicken and bake 30–40 minutes in 375° oven. Or, return chicken to skillet, cover, and simmer 40 minutes. Serve with rice.

CHICKEN NARANJA

breasts and thighs for 4
1 can frozen orange juice
2 tablespoons oil
2 tablespoons butter or
* margarine*
½ cup Pepperidge Farm Herb
* Seasoned Stuffing*

½ teaspoon each: salt, pepper,
* garlic powder*
1 teaspoon paprika
½ cup dry white wine
1 can small white onions
1 can artichoke hearts

Prepare orange juice according to directions on can and set aside. Brown chicken in oil and butter. While heat is medium high, add stuffing and turn chicken until stuffing is well distributed (scrape bottom of pan). Lower heat, add seasonings, turn chicken again, then add ½ cup orange juice and simmer 15 minutes. Add wine, drained onions and artichoke hearts. Cook 25 minutes longer, adding orange juice as needed to keep ample amount of gravy.

CHICKEN IN WINE SAUCE

2 broiler-fryers, 2–2½ pounds
  each
4 tablespoons butter
2 tablespoons oil
¾ cup chopped onions
½ cup Pepperidge Farm Herb
  Seasoned Stuffing

2 garlic cloves, minced
chopped parsley
salt and pepper
1 cup dry white wine
1 pound fresh mushrooms,
  whole (or 2 6-ounce cans)

Bone, disjoint, and sauté chicken in 2 tablespoons butter and 2 tablespoons oil. Add 2 more tablespoons butter and sauté onions until tender. Add stuffing mix, minced garlic, parsley, and seasoning, fry a few minutes longer, making sure to scrape all brown bits on bottom of skillet. Add wine, cook over low heat for 15 minutes, add mushrooms and cook 10 minutes longer or until chicken is tender. Serve with Noodle Toss (see p. 51).

CREAM CHEESE COOKIES

½ pound stick butter   2 cups flour, sifted
½ pound cream cheese   apricot preserves

Cream butter and cheese and gradually work in flour. Form
dough into 2 balls, wrap in waxed paper, and refrigerate at
least 2 hours. (Can be kept in refrigerator overnight.) On
floured board, roll out dough to approximately ⅛″ thick-
ness. Cut in squares, place spoonful of preserves in center
of each square, and fold corners toward center. Bake in
350° oven until golden brown (about 15–20 minutes).

On Board Recipes

Appetizers

CLAM DIP

1 can minced clams
1 package sour cream mix
⅓ cup milk
¼ cup mayonnaise

2 tablespoons dried minced
  onions
⅛ teaspoon garlic powder
⅛ teaspoon Jane's Krazy salt

Prepare sour cream mix according to instructions on package. Mix in rest of ingredients and let sit 5 or 10 minutes to improve flavor.

CRAB MEAT DIP

1 can crab meat
½ cup mayonnaise
½ cup chili sauce
1 tablespoon Worcestershire
  sauce

½ teaspoon garlic salt
2 hard-boiled eggs, chopped
½ teaspoon dried mustard
1 tablespoon horseradish
⅛ teaspoon tabasco sauce

Mix all above ingredients and chill.

For quick version of this dip on board, use crab meat, mayonnaise, chili sauce (or ketchup), garlic salt and Worcestershire sauce. Not quite as good, but almost.

DEVILED CRAB EGGS

6 hard-boiled eggs
1 can crab meat
4–5 heaping tablespoons
  mayonnaise
1 teaspoon dry mustard
1 tablespoon dried chopped
  chives

1 tablespoon dried minced
  onions
pinch garlic powder
few drops Worcestershire
  sauce
paprika
parsley flakes

Cut eggs in half lengthwise and remove yolks. In bowl, mash yolks, add next 7 ingredients and mix well. Fill egg whites with mixture and garnish with paprika and parsley flakes.

MOCK LIPTAUER CHEESE

1 8-ounce package Neufchatel
  cheese
5 tablespoons butter
2 tablespoons mustard

1 tablespoon mayonnaise
1 tablespoon pickle relish
1–2 tablespoons paprika

Combine softened butter with cheese. Add mustard, mayonnaise, relish, and paprika. Blend with fork until a soft, orangy cheese color. Use as spread or soften with sherry until desired consistency for dip.

MOZZARELLA DELIGHT

½ pound mozzarella
8 slices white bread
1 egg
1 tablespoon milk

butter
anchovy paste
¾ cup bread crumbs
oil

Trim bread crusts and cut each slice into quarters. Beat egg and milk in shallow bowl. Cut cheese in ¼"-thick slices and butter each slice of bread. Cover buttered bread with slice of cheese and make an X of anchovy paste on cheese. Top with another bread slice, buttered side down. Dip in beaten egg, then bread crumbs, and fry in oil. Garnish with rolled anchovy fillet. (Wonderful for cocktail parties at home!)

Soups

CHICKEN AND MUSHROOM GUMBO

2 cups cooked chicken or
   turkey, diced
2 6-ounce cans sliced
   mushrooms
3 tablespoons butter or
   margarine
2 cans undiluted chicken broth

½ cup Quick Rice
¼ teaspoon crumbled
   tarragon leaves
1 cup milk
salt
pepper

Drain mushrooms and reserve liquid. Sauté them in pot large enough to hold rest of ingredients. Add broth, bring to boiling point, add rice and tarragon, and cook for 5–10 minutes. Add chicken or turkey, milk, mushroom liquid and season to taste. Heat 5 minutes more. Serve with French bread and tossed green salad.

CHINESE GARDEN SOUP

1 can beef broth
1 divider-pak chicken chow
   mein or beef chop suey
   (16 ounce) and sauce

1 pound can tomatoes
½ teaspoon salt
¼ teaspoon pepper

Bring above ingredients to boiling point and simmer a few minutes. Serve with a sprinkling of chopped chives or croutons.

CRAB ALLEY CREAM

1 can crab meat (wash and
   drain)
1 10½-ounce can tomato soup
1 10½-ounce can pea soup
1 can (soup) water

½ pint cream or cream
   substitute
sherry to taste
1 tablespoon chopped chives

Mix soups and water and heat in pan, but do not boil. Add crab meat, then stir in cream or substitute. Heat again without boiling and add sherry immediately before serving. Garnish with chopped chives.

CRAB SOUP A LA FISHING CREEK

1 can king crab
1 can cream of celery soup
½ cup milk

⅓ cup sauterne
nutmeg

Heat crab meat, celery soup, milk, and wine until simmering. Serve with a sprinkling of nutmeg on each portion.

LEMON COOLER SOUP

1 10½-ounce can creamed
   chicken soup
2½ tablespoons water
2 teaspoons curry powder

1 cup cream substitute
6 tablespoons lemon juice
parsley flakes

Beat chicken soup and 1½ tablespoons water with egg beater. Mix curry powder with 1 tablespoon water and add to mixture. Blend in cream substitute with beater. Stir in lemon juice immediately before serving and garnish with parsley flakes.

LIGHTHOUSE SOUP

1 can condensed pea soup
1 can condensed potato soup
1½ cans milk

1 5-ounce can deviled ham or
   minced clams
chopped chives

Blend soups, 1½ (soup) cans of milk, and deviled ham.
Heat and serve with a sprinkling of chopped chives.

LILI'S FISH CHOWDER

1 can Snow's Fish Chowder
1 can minced clams
salt and pepper to taste
1 tablespoon dried chopped
   chives

¼-½ cup cream or cream
   substitute
butter

Combine chowder, minced clams, salt, pepper, and chives
and heat to boiling point. Lower heat and simmer a few
minutes. Turn off heat, stir in cream and pour into in-
dividual bowls. Serve with chunk of butter on each serving.

SALMON CHOWDER

1-pound can salmon
1 chicken bouillon cube
1 cup boiling water
2 tablespoons chopped onion
½ cup chopped green pepper
1 clove minced garlic
¼ cup butter or margarine
⅓ cup salmon liquid

1-pound can tomatoes
1 can (8-ounce) whole kernel
   corn
½ teaspoon salt
¼ teaspoon thyme
dash of pepper
1 whole bay leaf

Drain salmon, reserving liquid. Break salmon into large pieces. Dissolve bouillon cube in boiling water. Cook moistened onion, green pepper, and garlic in butter until tender. Combine all ingredients and cook for 15 minutes or until vegetables are tender. Remove bay leaf. Serves 6.

SHRIMP CHOWDER

1 5-ounce can shrimp, drained
   and rinsed
1 chopped onion
1½ cans (2 cups) water
1 tablespoon butter or
   margarine

1 can condensed cream of
   celery soup
1 can condensed clam chowder
1 tablespoon parsley flakes

Soak onion and drain excess water. Melt butter in saucepan and cook onion until tender. Blend in remaining ingredients and simmer for 5 minutes. Garnish with parsley.

TOMATO ORANGE SOUP

2 tablespoons butter or
   margarine
1 onion, diced
2 cans tomato soup

1 can unsweetened orange
   juice (16-ounce size)
salt and pepper
chopped chives

Melt butter or margarine in saucepan and brown onion. Add tomato soup and orange juice; heat but do not boil. Season to taste with salt and pepper. Garnish with chopped chives or croutons.

Eggs

DANISH BACON AND EGG CAKE

1 can prefried bacon
6 eggs
½ teaspoon Jane's Krazy Salt
1 tablespoon flour
½ cup milk

2 tablespoons butter or
   margarine
3 tablespoons dried chopped
   chives

Cut bacon strips in half and warm in 10″–12″ skillet. Do not let them get crisp. Set aside on paper towel. Put eggs, salt, and flour in mixing bowl; beat lightly (only long enough to combine them). Slowly beat in milk. Heat butter in skillet, pour in egg mixture and turn heat down to low. Without stirring, cover and let set until firm. This should take about 15 or 20 minutes. Garnish with bacon and chives.

EGG FOO YUNG

1 cup diced ham
2 tablespoons minced dried
   onions
½ can Chop Suey vegetables

½ teaspoon salt
5 eggs, beaten
3 tablespoons butter or
   margarine

Combine first 4 ingredients, then add beaten eggs. Melt butter and fry mixture over medium heat as you would an omelet. Serve with a green salad and French bread.

Pasta

BAMI GORENG

The same as Nasi Goreng (*see* p. 66) except prepared with fried noodles instead of rice.

Try using cooked green noodles and fry in 3 tablespoons butter or margarine. Add 2 tablespoons dried minced onion, ¼ teaspoon garlic salt, and ¼ teaspoon pepper.

FETTUCCINE

½ pound fettuccine, cooked and hot
¼ pound sweet butter

½ cup heavy sweet cream or cream substitute
½ cup Parmesan cheese
black pepper

Pour melted butter and cream over fettuccine; mix gently. Mix in grated cheese with black pepper. (Pasta should be hot enough to melt the cheese slightly.)

MACARONI WITH HAM AND EGGS

⅓ of a 1-pound box of elbow
macaroni
1 tablespoon butter or
margarine

½ cup ham cut in short
matchstick pieces
2 eggs
salt and pepper
grated Parmesan cheese

Cook macaroni "al dente," drain, and set aside in covered bowl. Melt butter in skillet and sauté the ham. Add slightly beaten eggs and seasonings and stir as you would for scrambled eggs. When eggs are just beginning to thicken, pour whole mixture over the hot macaroni. Stir well and sprinkle generously with the Parmesan cheese. Serve with more cheese on the side.

NOODLE TOSS

1 package thin noodles or
vermicelli
5–6 tablespoons butter

1 tablespoon minced dried
onion
2 tablespoons chopped chives
garlic salt and pepper to taste

Boil noodles. Drain, stir in butter until melted through. Add dried onions, chives, and seasonings and toss.

Meats

CANADIAN BACON WITH
APPLES AND ONIONS

3 tablespoons butter or
  margarine
1 pound Canadian bacon
2 large onions, thinly sliced

1 jar apple rings, or 2 apples,
  sliced
black pepper

Melt butter in heavy skillet, add bacon and fry until lightly browned. Remove and set aside on paper towel. Add more butter if necessary and fry onions until soft and transparent. Add apple rings and cover pan. Simmer for 5 minutes, return bacon to skillet, and simmer 5 minutes more. Serve with black pepper sprinkled on top. (If fresh tart apples are available, cut in ½″ rings and core but do not peel.)

BEEF VINAIGRETTE

2 cups canned beef
½ cup wine vinegar
½ cup olive oil
4 tablespoons capers (one
  small jar)
tabasco sauce
2 tablespoons dried parsley

¼ teaspoon dry mustard
2 tablespoons salad herbs, or
2 teaspoons each chervil,
  tarragon, dried chives
¼ teaspoon pepper
2 onions, sliced

Combine vinegar, oil, capers, tabasco sauce, herbs, and pepper in a bowl. Separate onion slices into rings and add to mixture along with the meat, which should be cut into strips or chunks. Toss and let stand "at boat temperature" one hour, then chill thoroughly. Serve over lettuce or *hot* rice.

BEEF RAGOUT

1 can Wilson's beef
3 tablespoons butter or
  margarine
2 tablespoons flour
1¾ cups water

1 envelope onion soup mix
¾ cup dry red wine
1 small can sliced mushrooms
1 small can white onions
1 can baby carrots

Melt butter in skillet and blend in flour. Add water a little
at a time, then the soup mix and wine. Stir over medium
heat until thickened. Discard juices from beef and cut beef
into chunks. Add meat and drained vegetables, heat through
and serve over noodles. Serves 6.

BEEF WITH WINE AND PICKLES

1 can Wilson's beef
2 onions, coarsely diced
oil
1 tablespoon paprika
¼ teaspoon garlic powder

¼ teaspoon pepper
1 can beef bouillon
1 cup dry red wine
2 tablespoons flour
½ cup sweet pickles

Brown onions lightly in oil. Add paprika, garlic, and pepper
and coat onions thoroughly. Add bouillon and wine and

bring to boil. Add meat, in chunks, and simmer 5 minutes. Take off ½ cup gravy and mix in flour; return to mixture and stir until gravy thickens slightly. Add sliced pickles, simmer 2 minutes longer and serve over noodles.

(Note: Discard juices when opening meat. Do not substitute for bouillon.)

IRISH BEEF STEW—BEEFED UP

2 cans Irish beef stew
½ cup dry red wine
2 tablespoons powdered beef
   bouillon (prime broth)

1 small can mushrooms
1 small can peas
1 small can white onions
2 tablespoons paprika

Drain vegetables. Heat all ingredients together and serve over noodles.

MEATBALLS IN HORSERADISH SAUCE

1 can meatballs
2 onions, sliced
2 tablespoons oil
1 tablespoon flour
½ teaspoon salt
¼ teaspoon pepper

½ bay leaf
¼ teaspoon dried thyme leaves
1 small can lima beans
1 cup tomato juice
1 tablespoon horseradish
⅓ cup sour cream

Brown onions in oil, then stir in flour, salt, pepper, bay leaf, thyme, and limas. Add tomato juice, bring to boil, cover, and simmer 25 to 30 minutes. Combine horseradish and sour cream and stir into sauce. Add meatballs (without gravy) and cook until heated through, but do not boil. Stir occasionally and remove bay leaf before serving.

STUFFED CABBAGE

2 cans S. S. Pierce stuffed
   cabbage
1-pound can stewed tomatoes

1 small can tomato paste
½ teaspoon garlic powder
oregano to taste

Combine all ingredients. Simmer 10 to 15 minutes and serve over rice.

SWEDISH HASH

½ can Wilson's roast beef
½ pound canned or boiled
  ham
2 cans white potatoes
2 tablespoonsful butter or
  margarine

2 tablespoons oil
1 onion, diced
salt and pepper
2 tablespoons parsley flakes
4 fried eggs

Dice meat and potatoes. Melt butter and oil in skillet and fry potatoes and onion until golden. Add meats and turn often until browned on all sides. Add salt and pepper to taste, sprinkle with parsley and serve with fried egg on top of each portion.

SWEET AND SOUR MEATBALLS

1 pound can meatballs in gravy
1 can (about 1 cup) pineapple
  tidbits
2 tablespoons cornstarch
¼ cup brown sugar

½ cup water
¼ cup cider vinegar
1 teaspoon soy sauce
1 5-ounce can water chestnuts
1 green pepper, diced

Drain pineapple, reserving syrup. Combine cornstarch and brown sugar in medium saucepan. Blend in syrup, water, vinegar, and soy sauce. Cook and stir until thickened, then stir in meatballs with gravy, sliced chestnuts, green pepper, and pineapple. Heat to boiling and serve over rice.

CURRIED HAM

2 cups cubed ham
1 tablespoon butter or
  margarine
1 diced onion
½ green pepper, diced
1 can condensed cream of
  celery soup

¾ cup milk
⅓ cup mayonnaise
1 small can sliced mushrooms,
  drained
½ teaspoon curry powder

Melt shortening in skillet and add onion and green pepper. Cook until tender but not brown. Stir in soup, milk, and mayonnaise. Add ham, mushrooms, and curry powder; cook and stir until heated through. Serve over rice.

HAM WITH CARY SAUCE

Sliced ham
1 can pitted dark bing cherries
2 teaspoons cornstarch

1 tablespoon minced candied
*   ginger*
2 tablespoons Grand Marnier

Drain cherries, reserving juice. Add enough water to juice
to make 1 cup. In saucepan, blend cornstarch with small
amount of the juice, add remaining juice, cherries, and ginger. Bring to boil; simmer 2 minutes. Add liqueur just before serving over hot or cold ham.

HAM 'N NOODLE SALAD

1 cup diced ham
1 cup medium egg noodles
3 hard-boiled eggs
2 tablespoons dried minced
   onion
¼ cup sweet pickles

1 small can water chestnuts,
   sliced
½ cup mayonnaise
1 tablespoon dried chives
salt and pepper to taste

Cook noodles according to directions on package. Drain and set aside. In large bowl, slice eggs, add minced onion, ham, sliced pickles, and chestnuts. Add noodles, mayonnaise, and seasonings and toss lightly until mayonnaise is well distributed.

A can of tuna or leftover chicken, meat, etc. can be substituted for ham.

SWEET AND SOUR HAM

1-pound can or 2 cups cubed
   ham
16 ounce can apricot halves
2 green peppers, diced
1 can chicken broth
⅓ cup sugar

¼ cup vinegar
3 tablespoons butter or
   margarine
3 tablespoons soy sauce
4 tablespoons cornstarch

Drain apricots and save syrup. Combine syrup, ham, diced peppers, approximately ¾ can of broth, sugar, vinegar, butter, and soy sauce in large saucepan. Bring to boil, cover, and simmer 10 minutes. Blend cornstarch with remaining broth and add to mixture. Stir constantly and boil 2 minutes. Add apricots and serve over rice.

PORK MARSALA

1 can Wilson's pork	½ cup Pepperidge Farm Herb
1 large onion, sliced	Seasoned Stuffing
2 tablespoons oil	½ cup Marsala wine
1 can sliced mushrooms	¼ cup raisins
½ teaspoon Jane's Krazy Salt	1 can orange juice (6-ounce
½ teaspoon tarragon	individual serving)
	1 cup peanuts or cashews

Brown onion in oil, adding mushrooms the last few minutes. Drain juice from meat, pat meat dry, cut into chunks, and brown on all sides. Add seasonings and stuffing mix while on high heat, scraping bottom and turning quickly until all ingredients are lightly browned. Add wine and raisins, cover and steam through 3 or 4 minutes. Add orange juice and nuts, heat 4 or 5 minutes more, and serve over rice. Serves 6.

PORK PIQUANT

1 can Wilson's pork
1 onion, sliced
1 green pepper, diced
oil for frying
1-pound can whole tomatoes
1-pound can Blue Lake whole
    green beans

½ teaspoon garlic powder
2 teaspoons sugar
½ teaspoon salt
½ teaspoon pepper
slivered almonds

Sauté onion and green pepper in oil. Add tomatoes, sugar, drained beans, seasonings, and meat (discard liquid). Simmer 15 to 20 minutes. Serve over rice and sprinkle with slivered almonds. Should serve 5 or 6 people.

PORK WITH WINE AND PICKLES

1 can Wilson's pork
1 onion, diced
2 tablespoons butter or
    margarine
2 tablespoons oil
1 tablespoon flour

salt and pepper to taste
½ can chicken broth
½ cup dry white wine
1 teaspoon wine vinegar
½ cup sweet gherkins
2 tablespoons sherry

Drain and dry pork and cut into chunks. Brown with onion in butter and oil. Remove meat from skillet. Sprinkle flour, salt, and pepper into pan and stir until brown. Add broth gradually, stirring constantly. Add wine, vinegar, and pickles and simmer a few minutes. Return meat to pan, simmer until heated through and add sherry. Should serve 5 or 6.

Fowl

CHICKEN BERCY

1 canned chicken
1 large can sliced mushrooms
1 tablespoon dried chopped
  chives
3 tablespoons butter or
  margarine

salt and pepper
¾ cup dry white wine
4 tablespoons butter or
  margarine
dried parsley flakes
¼ teaspoon garlic (optional)

Sauté mushrooms and chives in 3 tablespoons butter. Season with salt, pepper and garlic, add wine, and cook for 5 minutes on low heat. Remove from heat, add rest of butter, 1 tablespoon at a time, and return to burner. Add chicken (in parts or boned) and heat through. Sprinkle with parsley.

CHICKEN NICOISE

1 whole chicken, canned
1-pound can artichoke hearts
1 can pitted black olives
½ teaspoon garlic powder
3 tablespoons butter

½ cup dry white wine
1 teaspoon chopped tarragon
1-pound can tomatoes,
   chopped and drained
½ cup chicken broth

Sauté drained artichoke hearts, olives, and garlic in butter. Cook 1 minute, then add wine and tarragon. Cook a few minutes longer to reduce liquid, then add tomatoes and chicken broth and simmer 5 minutes. Add salt and pepper if desired. Add chicken, heat through and serve.

CHICKEN L'ORANGE

1 canned chicken
3 tablespoons butter or
   margarine
2 tablespoons flour
¼ teaspoon ginger

¼ teaspoon nutmeg
1 teaspoon salt
2 tablespoons currant jelly
1 cup canned orange juice

Melt butter and blend in flour. Add spices, salt, and jelly. Stir in orange juice, add chicken (in parts or boned), heat until thickened, and serve over rice.

CHUTNIED CHICKEN SALAD

2 cups cubed chicken
¾ cup mayonnaise
½ cup chutney
¼ cup dark raisins
½ cup salted peanuts
½ cup flaked coconut

½ teaspoon salt
2 bananas
1 avocado
3 tablespoons "Realemon"
    juice

Mix first 6 ingredients, then add salt. Slice bananas diagonally and cut avocado into lengthwise slices. Dip fruits in lemon juice and arrange around mounds of salad on lettuce leaves.

INSTANT CHICKEN CACCIATORA

1 5-ounce jar or can boned
   chicken
¼ teaspoon garlic powder
2 tablespoons dried chopped
   chives

¼ teaspoon oregano
1 8-ounce can Italian tomato
   sauce

Add garlic powder, chives, and oregano to tomato sauce. Bring to boil, then simmer for 10 minutes. Add chicken, heat through, and serve over thin spaghetti cooked "al dente." For variation, try serving with green noodles.

NASI GORENG

1 can Chun King Fried Rice
   with Pork
3 tablespoons butter or
   margarine

4 slices cooked ham
4 eggs
4 portions cooked chicken
1 can sliced tomatoes

Brown fried rice in shortening. Use one slice of ham per serving and cover with mound of rice. Top with fried egg. Serve with chicken to one side and tomatoes on the other. A hearty, *easy,* especially tasty dish for home as well as boat.

TURKEY CANTONESE

½ can Wilson's turkey
2 medium onions, sliced
1 6-ounce can sliced or whole
   mushrooms
2 green peppers, cut in large
   chunks
2 tablespoons butter or
   margarine

2 tablespoons oil
¼ teaspoon garlic powder
¼ teaspoon minced ginger
1 teaspoon soy sauce
2 teaspoons brown sugar
¼ cup dry white wine

Sauté onions, drained mushrooms, and green peppers in butter and oil. When golden brown, season with garlic, ginger, soy sauce, and sugar. Add wine and turkey chunks and simmer until heated through. Serve over rice or Chinese noodles.

TURKEY CURRY

1 can Wilson's turkey
½ stick margarine
4 tablespoons flour
¾ cup milk
1 can chicken broth

1 tablespoon curry powder
½ teaspoon ground ginger
  (optional)
2 tablespoons chutney
salt and pepper

Melt margarine, remove from heat and stir in flour. Gradually add milk, then broth. Heat until thickened, stirring constantly. Blend in curry, ginger, and chutney. Add chunks of turkey and stir until heated through. Correct seasoning with salt and pepper and serve over rice with 3 or 4 condiments. (Always chutney and raisins; chopped eggs, crumbled bacon left over from breakfast, sliced water chestnuts, etc.) Recipe can also be made with chicken, lamb, or veal. Serves 5–6.

Fish

ARTICHOKE CRAB ORIENTAL

2 jars marinated artichoke
   hearts
1 can king crab
½ cup water
1 tablespoon cornstarch

½ cup soy sauce
1 tablespoon sugar
2 hard-boiled eggs
1 can mushrooms
freeze-dried chives

Put water in saucepan and stir in cornstarch. Add soy sauce and sugar and stir constantly over low heat until thickened. Place crab and artichokes on rice mounds, pour sauce mixture over, and garnish with sliced eggs, mushrooms, and chives.

CRAB A LA KING

1 can crab meat
4 tablespoons margarine
1 small can sliced mushrooms
½ green pepper
3 tablespoons flour

1 teaspoon salt
¼ teaspoon pepper
½ cup cream substitute
1 cup milk
1 tablespoon lemon juice

Melt margarine. Add mushrooms, sliced green pepper, and cook a few minutes. Stir in flour and seasonings. Add cream substitute and milk gradually, stirring constantly. Beat in lemon juice and add drained crab meat. Heat again and serve over rice or Holland Rusk. Sprinkle each serving with paprika and parsley flakes for color.

CRAB-BURGERS

1 pound crab meat, or
  2 8-ounce cans
1 cup bread crumbs
1 egg
¼ cup mayonnaise
2 teaspoons prepared mustard

1 teaspoon Worcestershire
  sauce
½ teaspoon salt
¼ teaspoon pepper
oil for frying

Mix bread crumbs, egg, mayonnaise, mustard, and seasonings in bowl. Work in crab meat (be sure meat is throughly shelled) and shape into cakes. Brown in oil and serve with tartar sauce.

CRAB MEAT CREOLE

1 6½-ounce king crab meat
1 large onion, sliced
1 green pepper, diced
3 tablespoons oil
1 No. 2½ can tomatoes
2 tablespoons dried parsley
½ teaspoon gumbo filé

½ teaspoon garlic powder
2 teaspoons paprika
1 tablespoon dried chives
½ cup ketchup
1 can water chestnuts
salt and pepper to taste

Brown onion and green pepper in oil. Lower heat, add tomatoes, spices, and ketchup and simmer 15 minutes. Add crab meat, sliced water chestnuts and heat a few minutes longer. Serve over rice.

DOLPHIN AU GRATIN

Fish fillets for 4
1 tablespoon butter or
    margarine
1 tablespoon oil
¼ teaspoon each salt and
    pepper
¼ teaspoon garlic powder

½ teaspoon paprika
2 tablespoons dried chives
¾ cup Pepperidge Farm Herb
    Seasoned Stuffing
½ cup dry white wine (or
    grapefruit or orange juice)

Brown both sides of fillets in butter and oil and season with salt, pepper, garlic, paprika, and chives. While flame is high, add bread stuffing and turn fillets a few times, making sure to scrape bottom of pan. Lower flame, add wine, and cover pan. Simmer about 5 minutes or until the fish flakes. Add water if needed to keep moist with small amount of gravy. (*See* page 74 for "Fish Salad Supreme" for leftovers.)

LOBSTER OR CRAB NEWBURG
(The longer way)

2 cans crab or lobster
2 tablespoons butter or
    margarine
2 teaspoons lemon juice
¼ cup dry sherry

1½ cups light cream or cream
    substitute
3 egg yolks
salt and nutmeg to taste

Cut fish into bite-sized chunks. Sauté lightly in heated butter, then remove from burner and sprinkle with lemon juice and wine. Heat about 2 minutes. Add cream and heat just to simmering; do not boil. Beat egg yolks lightly and mix in a few spoonfuls of the hot cream. Stir into rest of cream (with meat) and cook, stirring constantly, until sauce thickens lightly (not thick and heavy). Add salt and nutmeg. Serve in patty shells and sprinkle with paprika.

MINUTE LOBSTER
OR SHRIMP NEWBURG

2 cans shrimp or lobster
1 can Milani's Newburg Sauce

½ teaspoon nutmeg
¼ cup sherry

Heat sauce with nutmeg and rinsed shrimp or lobster. Do not boil. Add sherry right before serving and serve over hot rice.

FISH FRY

Fish fillets for 4
2 eggs
2 tablespoons prepared
  mustard
½ teaspoon Jane's Krazy
  Mixed-up Salt

mashed potato flakes
2 tablespoons butter or
  margarine
1 tablespoon oil
dried chopped chives

In shallow dish, beat eggs with mustard and Jane's Salt. Dip fillets in egg mixture, then in potato flakes. Fry in butter and oil until golden brown and the fish flakes—about five or six minutes. Garnish with chives.

FISH SALAD SUPREME

2 cups cold fish "au Gratin"
  (See p. 71)
1 green pepper, diced
2 heaping tablespoons dried
  minced onions
3–4 scallions, sliced

5–6 canned water chestnuts,
  sliced
½ teaspoon Jane's Krazy
  Mixed-up Salt
4 tablespoons mayonnaise
1 tablespoon salad oil
2 tablespoons vinegar

Toss fish with pepper, onions, scallions, water chestnuts, and Jane's Salt. Combine mayonnaise, oil, and vinegar in separate cup, add to fish and toss again lightly. Serve with canned sliced tomatoes sprinkled with Jane's Salt and chives.

SALMON CROQUETTES

1 6½-ounce can salmon
2 eggs
2 tablespoons dried minced
  onion

½ teaspoon salt
¼ teaspoon pepper
bread crumbs or cracker meal
3 tablespoons oil or butter

Mash salmon in bowl. Mix in eggs, onions, salt and pepper. Let stand about 5 minutes. Add bread crumbs or cracker meal gradually until thick enough to form patties. Fry in oil or butter and serve with chili sauce or tartar sauce.

SALMON CURRY

1-pound can salmon	*1½ teaspoons curry powder*
1 tablespoon chopped onion	*½ teaspoon salt*
3 tablespoons butter or	*¼ teaspoon ginger*
margarine	*dash pepper*
3 tablespoons flour	*2 cups salmon liquid and milk*

Drain salmon, reserving liquid, and break into large pieces. Cook moistened onion in butter until yellow, then blend in flour and seasonings. Gradually add salmon liquid (with enough milk to make 2 cups) and cook until thick, stirring constantly. Add salmon and heat through. Serve over rice with any of the following condiments: chopped nuts, shredded coconut, chopped tomatoes, fried noodles (canned), etc. Serves 6.

SEAFOOD TREASURE

1 can shrimp	1 teaspoon each: basil,
1 can crab meat	tarragon, chervil
1 can lobster	½ teaspoon garlic powder
1 onion, diced	salt and pepper to taste
1 8-ounce can sliced	4 ounces Cheese Whiz
mushrooms, drained	6 ounces mayonnaise (about
1 tablespoon dried chives	¾ of an 8-ounce jar)

Sauté onion and mushrooms. Lower heat; add drained and rinsed seafood. Add seasonings, then mix in Cheese Whiz and mayonnaise. Heat through over low flame, stirring often. Serve over rice and garnish with paprika and chives.

SHRIMP JAMBALAYA

2 cans shrimp	1¼ cups water
½ cup diced ham	2 tablespoons minced onion
2 tablespoons oil	¼ teaspoon pepper
1 green pepper, diced	½ teaspoon garlic salt
1-pound can tomatoes	1½ cups Quick Rice
1 can sliced mushrooms	

Sauté ham in oil. Add green pepper (diced) and cook a few minutes until tender. Add tomatoes, mushrooms, water, onion, and seasonings; cook 15 or 20 minutes. Add rice and shrimp, cook a few minutes longer, then cover and let stand 5 minutes before serving.

SHRIMP CALIBOGUE

2 cans medium or large shrimp
¼ pound butter or margarine
1 jar cocktail sausages
1-pound can seasoned green
  beans
¼ cup dry white wine
1 2-ounce jar pimientos

1 tablespoon dried minced
  onion
1 tablespoon freeze dried
  chives
⅛ teaspoon garlic powder
salt and pepper to taste

Melt 2 tablespoons butter in skillet and brown drained sausages. Drain green beans, reserving ¼ cup of the liquid. Lower heat, add green beans and the ¼ cup liquid, rinsed shrimp, remainder of butter, wine, and seasonings. Simmer another 3 or 4 minutes and correct seasoning, if needed.

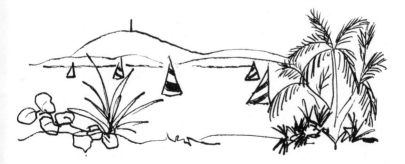

SHRIMP CURRY

2 cans shrimp
1 teaspoon curry powder
1 cup mayonnaise (8-ounce
  jar)
1 5½-ounce can evaporated
  milk

2 tablespoons pimiento
1 tablespoon chopped chives
2 tablespoons dried minced
  onions

Blend curry powder into mayonnaise. Gradually stir in evaporated milk, then add rest of ingredients. Heat and serve over rice.

TUNA, CHEESE, AND NOODLES

2 cans tuna fish
¾ box medium noodles
4 tablespoons margarine
  (or butter)

½ cup shredded Swiss cheese
¼ teaspoon pepper
1 small can peas
2 tablespoons chopped chives

Boil noodles in salted water. Drain noodles, add margarine (or butter), cheese, pepper, and mix. Add chunks of tuna, then peas. Sprinkle with chopped chives and serve.

ORIENTAL TUNA

1 6-ounce can tuna
2 tablespoons oil or margarine
1 onion, sliced
1 green pepper, diced
cold water
1 bouillon cube (beef)

¼ teaspoon salt
¼ teaspoon pepper
1 teaspoon cornstarch
1 teaspoon soy sauce
1 can Chinese noodles
slivered almonds

Drain and flake tuna. In skillet, lightly sauté onion and green pepper. Add water, heat 3 or 4 minutes, then add bouillon cube, salt and pepper. Blend cornstarch with 1 tablespoon cold water and soy sauce and stir into mixture in skillet. Bring to boil (stirring constantly) add tuna and sliced water chestnuts, heat through and serve over rice with crisp noodles and almonds.

Side Dishes

ASPARAGUS SALAD

1 can asparagus spears,
  drained
2 tablespoons dried minced
  onions
water

2 tablespoons salad oil
3 tablespoons tarragon vinegar
1 tablespoon freeze-dried
  chives
salt and pepper

Cover 2 tablespoons dried minced onions with water and let stand 5 minutes. Drain off any excess water. Add 2 tablespoons salad oil, 2 tablespoons tarragon vinegar, 1 tablespoon freeze-dried chives, salt and pepper; blend. Add one can drained asparagus spears and toss gently.

BACON DUMPLINGS

1 can prefried bacon
3 tablespoons butter or
  margarine
1½ cups bread cubes
1 tablespoon dried minced
  onion

1 tablespoon freeze dried
  chives
½ cup milk
1 tablespoon parsley flakes
½ cup flour
salt

Heat bacon in skillet. Remove and set aside on paper towel. Add butter to skillet, brown bread cubes and remove to mixing bowl. Add onion, chives, milk, and parsley to cubes. Cut bacon into small pieces and mix into bowl. Stir in flour

80

and set aside 5 or 10 minutes. Dampen hands, form into 1"–2" balls, drop into boiling salted water and cook about 15 minutes. Serve with meat and gravy. (Or, top with sauerkraut and add a can of fried onion rings for a main dish.)

BEAN SALAD SEVERN

1 small can cut green beans
1 small can cut wax beans
1-pound can red kidney beans
2 tablespoons minced onion

¼ cup salad oil
¼ cup vinegar
2 tablespoons chopped chives
salt and pepper

Drain vegetables, combine all ingredients and toss. No need to moisten onion beforehand. Just as good or better the second day and will keep for a week.

BEANS TORTOLA

1 can Boston baked beans
  (small pea size)
2 tablespoons sugar

1 tablespoon mustard
2 rounded tablespoons
  marmalade

Mix all ingredients and stir often while heating.

SWEET POTATO BALLS

1 can sweet potatoes
2 tablespoons margarine
¼ teaspoon salt

1 egg
marshmallows
corn flakes

Drain and mash sweet potatoes, adding margarine, salt, and egg. Make patties of mixture and wrap each around a marshmallow to form a ball. Dip in crushed corn flakes and fry in deep fat or oil.

Breads

UPSIDE DOWN CORNBREAD

4 tablespoons butter or
    margarine
1 small can sliced pineapple

1 can prefried bacon
1 package cornbread mix

Melt butter in skillet. Remove pan from burner and arrange
pineapple and half of bacon on bottom of skillet. Prepare
cornbread mix according to directions on package and pour
over bacon and pineapple. Cover and cook over low heat
15 to 20 minutes or until test fork or toothpick comes out
dry. Serve upside down with pancake syrup and other half
of bacon on the side.

Try substituting Canadian bacon and peach halves for
variety.

Desserts

BROWN BETTY A LA CHESAPEAKE

1 can sliced apples
2 tablespoons butter
1 tablespoon sugar

½ teaspoon cinnamon
1 cup corn flakes, crushed
cream or cream substitute

Heat canned sliced apples and divide into 4 dishes. Melt 2 tablespoons butter. Add 1 tablespoon sugar, ½ teaspoon cinnamon and 1 cup crushed corn flakes. Divide over apples and serve with cream or cream substitute.

SHIPSHAPE FRUIT DESSERT

1-pound can or jar of
applesauce
1 30-ounce can fruit cocktail,
drained

1 5½-ounce jar McCormick's
Cinnamon Decors

Cook applesauce, fruit salad, and Cinnamon Decors over low heat until candies are melted. Serve hot or cold. (Makes wonderful cold snack, too.) Dab of whipped cream or dessert topping optional.

Dessert Tips

The most convenient, stowable desserts to take aboard seem to take the form of packaged cakes and cookies. Frozen cakes defrost and maintain their freshness up to 2 weeks in the galley icebox. If there is time before the weekend or the start of a longer trip, there are few delights more pleasing to the skipper than a plastic container of Cream Cheese Cookies (recipe on page 36) or one of your own favorite cookie recipes. But among the easiest, most refreshing, and possibly more healthful desserts to carry are canned fruits. The following suggestions include a few ways to spruce up canned fruits, as well as other tips to add variety to your dessert menu.

Pour 1 or 2 tablespoons of sherry, cognac, or other liqueur over pear halves.

Crumble macaroons over peach halves with a dash of liqueur.

Drain red, tart, pitted cherries and heat with currant jelly. Add cognac and serve over pears.

Mandarin oranges and bite-sized marshmallows sprinkled with cocoanut.

Make your own fruit salad combinations from canned fruit. For example: Pineapple chunks, strawberries, and mandarin oranges; grapefruit sections with dark bing cherries; boysenberries, pineapple, and sliced pears.

Sprinkle chopped dates and nuts over peaches or pears.

Sprinkle shredded cocoanut over mandarin oranges and sliced bananas.

Serve pear halves with chocolate syrup and nuts.

Spread canned date and nut bread with pineapple cheese (from jars).

Sprinkle frosted cereal flakes over peaches, pears, or apricots and serve with cream substitute.

Using pear and peach halves to substitute for ice cream, add bananas, pineapple preserves, chocolate fudge sauce, and walnuts. Pile on a fluffy white whipped topping mix, chopped nuts, and a maraschino cherry for a great imitation banana split.

Flavor a whipped topping mix with a tablespoon or two of your favorite liqueur and serve over slices of canned chocolate nut loaf or fruit and nut loaf.

Beverages

HOT BUTTERED RUM

In each mug, mix 1 tablespoon dark brown sugar, a dash of nutmeg, and 1 jigger of Jamaica rum. Fill with boiling water and add 1 tablespoon butter. Stir until butter is melted and add a cinnamon stick.

Index

Index